The Evolution

of

The Canterbury Tales.

The Evolution of
The Canterbury Tales.

BY THE

REV. WALTER W. SKEAT,

LITT.D., LL.D., D.C.L., PH.D., F.B.A.,

Elrington and Bosworth Professor of Anglo-Saxon in the University
of Cambridge, and Fellow of Christ's College.

HASKELL HOUSE PUBLISHERS LTD.
Publishers of Scarce Scholarly Books

NEW YORK. N. Y. 10017

1968

First Published 1907

HASKELL HOUSE PUBLISHERS Ltd.
Publishers of Scarce Scholarly Books
280 LAFAYETTE STREET
NEW YORK. N. Y. 10012

Library of Congress Catalog Card Number: 68-24919

Haskell House Catalogue Item # 240

The
Evolution of the Canterbury Tales.

Table 1.	Knight, &c.	(1) Wife, &c.	(1) Shipman, &c.	(1) Maniciple.	(**Table 2** *follows*).
Hengwrt	1	3	7b*	9a	
A. Petworth	1				
B. Lansdowne *	1				* *also* Corpus.
C. Harleian	1				
C*. Ellesmere †	1				† *also* Cambridge.

Table 2.	Man of Law.	Sq. Prol. I.	(1) Squire.	Merch. Prol.	(1) Merchant.	(1) Frank. Prol.	(1) Franklin.	(2) Wife, &c.	(1) Sec. Nun.
Hengwrt	2		5a	n	4b	x, y	5b		8a
A. Petworth	2	m	5a	n	4b			3	
B. Lansdowne	2	m	5a	o				3	
C. Harleian	2	m						3	
C*. Ellesmere	2	o						3	

1. Prol., Knight, Miller, Reeve, Cook.
2. Man of Law.
3. Wife, Friar, Sompnour.
4a. Clerk.
4b. Merchant.
5a. Squire.
5b. Franklin.

6. Doctor, Pardoner.
7a. Shipman, Prioress, Sir Thopas, Melibee.
7b. Monk, Nun's Priest.
8a. Second Nun.
8b. Canon's Yeoman.
9a. Maniciple.
9b. Parson.

(1) Wife, etc. ; *i. e.* Wife, etc., *first position.* And so on.

Tables 1–4 are continuous.

Table 3.	Clerk.	Host-stanza.	Cl. Mer. link.	(2) Merchant.	Sq. Prol. II.	(2) Squire.	Words of Frank.	(2) Frank. Prol.	(2 Franklin.
Hengwrt	4a	h							
A. Petworth	4a	...	...	...	...	...	...	x, y	5b
B. Lansdowne	4a	o	o	4b				?	5b
C. Harleian ..., ...	4a	o	z	4b	x, y	5a	n	......	5b
C*. Ellesmere	4a	h	z	4b	x, y	5a	n	......	5b

Table 4.	(2) Doctor, &c.	(3) Shipman, &c.	(2) N.P. Epilogue.	(2) Sec. Nun, &c.	(1) Doctor, &c.	(2) Shipman, &c.	(1) N.P. Epilogue.	(2) Manciple.	Parson.
Hengwrt					6	7a			9b
A. Petworth				8	6	7	e	9a	9b
B. Lansdowne				8	6	7	o	9a	9b
C. Harleian				8	6	7	o	9a	9b
C*. Ellesmere	6	7*	e	8				9a	9b

m. Squire's Prol. (B 1163–1190). *m.* nameless Prol. (same lines).
n. Merch. Prol. (F 673–708). *n.* Words of Franklin (same lines).
h. Host-stanza (end of Clerk).
x, y. Franklin's Prol. (E 2419–F 8).
x. Merch. Epilogue ; *y.* Squire's Prol. (same lines as x, y).
z. Clerk-Merch. link (E 1213–1244).
e. Nun's Priest's Epilogue (B 4637–4652).
o. *i. e.* suppressed.
7*, or 7b.* Monk's Tale ends with Ugolino.

Tables 1–4 are continuous.

The
Evolution of the Canterbury Tales.

(Read at a Meeting of the Philological Society, Nov. 1, 1907.)

In the excellent Temporary Preface to Chaucer's Canterbury Tales, issued by Dr. Furnivall in 1868, the question as to the right arrangement of the Tales is carefully discussed; and the result arrived at was sufficient for the purpose. That purpose was, to place the Tales in the order in which Chaucer might have arranged the Tales himself, if he had lived to complete the work.

Dr. Furnivall showed that the Tales can be divided into about nine distinct groups. Those that occur within the same group are clearly linked together by the help of additional lines, occurring between the Tales, that serve to dismiss one Tale and to introduce another. In other words, there is no evidence that any of the arrangements in the manuscripts is final. All that can be said is that some arrangements are preferable to others; and the arrangement made by Dr. Furnivall is suitable for practical purposes.

What I now propose to discuss is not quite the same problem. I have no wish to propose any arrangement of my own, or to form any theory at all beyond such as is borne out by the evidence. My purpose is purely historical, viz., to show that we have evidence for at least four different arrangements or schemes, and we are able to determine quite clearly how these four schemes came into being. They represent the Tales in four different stages, so to speak; and each depends, as of course it must depend, upon the scheme that preceded it. Whether such schemes are due to Chaucer himself, or to scribes, we shall see as we proceed. One at least of them is due to an editor, but the rest may well be his own. It is very difficult for any one accustomed only to printed books to realise what happened in

5

75-03736

the days of manuscripts. In the case of Langland's poem of Piers the Plowman, we have at least five forms in which the poem appears, not counting others which are obviously absurd. Of these five forms, three are due to the fact that the poem was twice rewritten ; this gives us at once an A-text, a B-text, and a C-text ; and it is now being maintained, not without reason, that this implies at least two authors, since the author of text B appears to have misunderstood some of the expressions used by the author of A. Besides these three texts, we have two more, certainly due to the mistakes of scribes ; for there is a set of manuscripts that contains a mixture of the A and C types, both imperfect, and unintelligently combined, and another unintelligent combination of the B and C types, likewise imperfect. We thus have positive evidence that the scribes who were employed to multiply manuscripts frequently did precisely as they pleased. They copied what they could come by ; and, if they could not get a perfect copy, they copied an imperfect one, completing it by help of another without considering whether it belonged, so to speak, to the same recension or not. Nothing can be more misleading than to apply ideas derived from the habits of modern printing to times when the very idea of printing was unknown. Just as we should expect to find printed copies, at the present day, resembling each other very much or altogether, we ought to expect the very contrary in the days when every copy was produced separately. Even if a reader dictated aloud to six copyists at once, each of these had, to say the least, his own ideas of spelling, or even of rhythm or of grammatical expression.

These preliminary remarks are absolutely necessary before any explanation is possible. Having made them, I propose to show that there are four main schemes of arrangement of the Canterbury Tales, neglecting, with one remarkable exception, the manuscripts in which no particular order has been observed.

For I propose to show, beforehand, that we actually possess one MS. which may be fairly regarded as approaching to the idea of an archetype; a MS., namely, in which the Groups of tales appear, at first sight, to take quite a casual order ; a MS. in which they may have been committed to writing with a view to future re-arrangement. By such re-arrangement we must, of course, construct a scheme that is necessarily the *oldest* of the four more orderly schemes, from which also, in turn, each of the

later schemes can be naturally developed, in regular succession.
The MS. to which I refer is the Hengwrt MS., which must, in
any case, be considered, since it is generally agreed that it is, with
one exception, the best we possess, at any rate as regards the
grammatical forms.

The Hengwrt MS. of the Canterbury Tales.

The Hengwrt MS. of the Canterbury Tales is known to be one
of the best. It stands second among the seven MSS. selected and
printed by the Chaucer Society. An examination of its contents
shows that it is unique, not only in the arrangement of the Tales
but in particulars relating to the Tales themselves.

I believe it can be explained as showing the Tales in their
oldest known condition. It represents, so to speak, a form of
them in which the idea of arrangement was quite imperfect; and
it was written out, probably with a view to future use, as a sort
of working copy. In fact, Dr. Furnivall noted, in 1868, that it
is "the least handsome of our six MSS., the least formally
written." But it may be a late copy of a MS. of a similar
kind. We should naturally expect it to be incomplete; and
indeed, its omissions are significant.

I suppose few remarks have been more frequently made than
this, viz. that the idea of the Canon's Yeoman was an afterthought. There is no hint of his existence in the General
Prologue; and the idea of inserting him among the rest did not
occur to the author till he had made considerable progress with
his work. It is highly probable, as has often been said, that
Chaucer suddenly discovered that he had something satirical to
say about the doings of the alchemists; and the ingenious way in
which the number of the pilgrims is said to have been enlarged
by the addition of the Canon and his Yeoman is almost beyond
praise. The thought was most happy and successful.

Now the Hengwrt MS. is so antique in its type that it knows
nothing of either the Canon or his Yeoman. All that we find is
the rubric: " Here is ended the Nonnes tale," on leaf 173. We
turn the leaf, and find, to our amazement, the Prologue to the
Clerkes Tale, which ought perhaps to have come in earlier, but
did not.

Another remarkable point is the absence, in its due place, of

the Tale of Melibeus, which nearly every other MS. and all
the printed editions put in its proper place, between Sir Thopas
and the Monk's Tale. But this MS. divides Group 7 into two
parts, giving the two last tales (the Monk and Nun's Priest) pre-
cedence, and relegating all the rest to a position just before the
Parson. And this is done in spite of the reference in the line—
"When ended was my tale of Melibee"—with which the Monk's
Prologue rightly begins.

A more important fact is that in this MS. (as in MS. Rawl.
Misc. 1133), the Manciple's Tale appears quite early, instead of
just before the Parson's Tale, as usual. Accordingly we find, in
the Prologue of the Parson's Tale, that the first line is :—" By
that the *Manciple* hadde his tale al ended," with a note to say
that *Manciple* is written over an erasure; *i. e.* it is not the
original reading, though nearly all other MSS. have it.

The Hengwrt MS. also preserves the old original seven-line
stanza at the end of the Clerk's Tale, printed in the note to my
edition, vol. iv. p. 424, and in the Student's Chaucer, p. 611.
I call this stanza the Host-stanza, and denote it in the Tables
above by " h." The conjecture that it was meant to follow
Group E, l. 1162, or l. 1169, is a conjecture, and nothing else.
If we are to go by evidence, its right place is after l. 1212. See
the Six-text edition, p. 477.

The conjecture was of course due to the inadvisability of
separating the words "wringe and wayle" in l. 1212 from
" Weping and wayling" in l. 1213 ; but this does not apply to
the Hengwrt MS. at all, because ll. 1213–1244 *do not occur in it*.

The Hengwrt MS. (followed here by the Corpus MS.) omits
the stanza on Adam in the Monk's Tale ; but this may have
been accidental. It does not greatly matter.

Another interesting point about this MS. is that, in the
Monk's Tale, the " modern " stories of the two Pedros, Visconti,
and Ugolino of Pisa are simply added at the *end* of the Tale,
though in the later schemes (except the Ellesmere, which is
unauthorised) they occur much earlier, as the case requires.
This is just what we should expect. We have, in the Hengwrt,
a nearer approach to the *actual* or original order, as regards date
of composition ; in the other schemes, we have a revised order,
written with a new intention. The placing of the modern stories
at the end does not contradict what is said in the Nun's Priest's

Prologue, because lines 3961–80 of Group B *do not appear* in the Hengwrt MS.

Another point is that there is in this MS. no Tale of Gamelin. It is possible that this Tale had not, as yet, attracted Chaucer's attention.

Once more. The Hengwrt MS. contains two additional lines in the Prologue, in the description of the Frere; ll. 252 *b, c.* But in the very first recension they were cut out or omitted, and therefore cannot be found in any other MS.

When once the antiquity of type of the Hengwrt MS. is understood, it presents no difficulty. It contains, in fact, ten groups instead of eight, owing to its insufficient arrangement.

The statement, just made, that the Hengwrt MS. contains ten groups requires explanation, because it seems, at first sight, to contain twelve. But the fact is that it joins together three tales which were afterwards re-arranged, viz. the Squire, the Merchant, and the Franklin. At the end of the Squire's Tale, we find the Merchant's Prologue (F 673–708), which is joined on to the preceding Squire's Tale by the first line, viz. "In faith, Squyer, thou hast thee wel y-quyt;" and the same arrangement continues in the Petworth scheme. (The ultimate fate of what is here called the Merchant's Prologue will be fully explained hereafter, when we come to speak of the Petworth MS.) Once more, the Merchant's Tale is followed by The Words of the Host to the Franklin (E 2419–2440) and by a Franklin's Prologue (F 1–8) and the Franklin's Tale. This reduces the number of groups to eleven; but it is really only ten, as group 7 has been casually divided into two parts.

I shall proceed to show that the chronological order of the types of the seven chief MSS., with reference, that is to say, to their contents and arrangement, but without regard to the actual dates when these individual MSS. were written, is as follows:— Hengwrt, an archetype; Petworth, showing the first scheme of arrangement; Corpus and Lansdowne, the second; Harleian, the third; Ellesmere and Cambridge, the fourth and last. In the first three schemes, we find Chaucer himself at work, making various experiments. In the last scheme, we find the work of a careful editor. It follows that the authoritative type, the only one which arranges the Tales as Chaucer at last left them, is the Harleian. It is anything but final, and even some obvious mistakes remain. But we have *no authority* for proceeding further.

I wish to state expressly that, in speaking of any MS. such as the Hengwrt, I do not refer so much to the MS. *itself* as to its *type* or scheme of arrangement. Neither do I in any way interfere with or contradict the arrangement into *seven groups*, as deduced by Dr. Koch from the readings of the MSS. in the extremely valuable Introduction to his edition of the Pardoner's Tale (Berlin, 1902). A group, as formed by MSS. which have similar readings, is quite a different thing from a type as deduced from the order in which the Tales are arranged. It is obvious that a type may include two or more groups.

For example, Dr. Koch places the Ellesmere MS. in Group I, and the Cambridge MS. in Group II ; no doubt, correctly. But the arrangement of the Tales is the same in both.

The Scheme of the Order of the Canterbury Tales, according to the Petworth MS.

In order to exhibit the arrangement of the Canterbury Tales as concisely as possible, it is best to adopt the notation employed by Dr. Furnivall in the Tables of MSS. prefixed to his Six-text edition of the Tales. I merely use arabic numerals in place of his roman ones.

The chief sets are as follows :—1. Prologue ; Knight ; Miller ; Reeve ; Cook.—2. Man of Law.—3. Wife ; Friar ; Sompnour.— 4*a*. Clerk ; 4*b*. Merchant.—5*a*. Squire ; 5*b*. Franklin.—6. Doctor ; Pardoner.—7*a*. Shipman ; Prioress ; Sir Thopas ; Melibee ; 7*b*. Monk ; Nun's Priest.—8*a*. Second Nun ; 8*b*. Canon's Yeoman.— 9*a*. Manciple ; 9*b*. Parson.

Let us first of all ascertain the order of the Tales in the Hengwrt MS. According to the above list, it is as follows, viz. 1. 3. 7*b*. 9*a*. 2. 5*a*. 4*b*. 5*b*. 8*a*. 4*a*. 6. 7*a*. 9*b*. See pp. 2, 3.

Moreover, the MS. makes it quite clear that 7*b* was destined to succeed 7*a*, though for some temporary reason it was placed earlier in this particular copy. It is best to make this alteration at once, which gives, as the true scheme for this MS., the arrangement :—1. 3. 9*a*. 2. 5*a*. 4*b*. 5*b*. 8*a*. 4*a*. 6. 7. 9*b*.

We see that, despite the apparent disorder, much has already been achieved. For Group 1 contains the Prologue and 4 Tales, all linked together ; Group 3 contains 3 Tales ; Group 6 contains 2 Tales ; and Group 7 no less than 6 Tales. *Not one of these groupings was afterwards disturbed.*

The next scheme, in chronological order, is one that appears in many MSS., with which the Petworth MS. very nearly agrees. I call it the Petworth scheme for convenience, though the Petworth MS. itself has one useless deviation from the rest, in that it places the Shipman and Prioress in front of the Man of Law instead of making them form part of Group 7.   This peculiarity may be neglected, as in other MSS. of the same type ; and we then observe the order of Tales to be : 1. 2. 5a. 4b. 3. 4a. 5b. 8. 6. 7. 9.

In spite of the great apparent difference between this and the Hengwrt MS., it is possible to bring the Hengwrt scheme into harmony with this by help of three displacements or removals. Thus the Hengwrt MS. has the order above :—1. 3. 9a. 2. 5a. 4b. 5b. 8a. 4a. 6. 7. 9b.   First place 3 after 4b ; this gives : 1. 9a. 2. 5a. 4b. 3. 5b. 8a. 4a. 6. 7. 9b.   Secondly, place 4a before 5b, and 9a before 9b. This gives :—1. 2. 5a. 4b. 3. 4a. 5b. 8a. 6. 7. 9a. 9b ; which is the Petworth order, all but 8b, which has still to be supplied. We know from the first line of the Canon's Yeoman's Prologue, that it was written to follow the Second Nun ; and when Group 8 was thus formed, it was never afterwards disturbed.

The mere shifting of detached groups is of course of no value in itself, unless it leads to something further. We have therefore to enquire whether anything else was done at the same time. We shall see presently that something has been gained, and that some attempt has been made towards the establishment of new connexions.

The Petworth scheme begins with 1, 2, 5a. Observe that most of the MSS. of this type insert the Tale of Gamelin after Group 1.   We can hardly doubt that this Tale was intended to provide material for a future Yeoman's Tale ; but we know, to our loss, that no such Tale was written.

Let us next consider the sequence 2, 5a ; the Man of Law and the Squire.   In the Hengwrt scheme we have the same sequence, though the two Tales are left disconnected. But in the Petworth scheme there is an attempt to join them together ; and, although this idea was afterwards abandoned, it is absolutely necessary to a right understanding of the MSS. that we should strictly look to what was done.

For, if we now turn to the end of the Man of Law's Tale, we find here a new Squire's Prologue, of which the Hengwrt MS. gave us no hint. It merely placed the Squire's Tale next, and nothing more. But the Petworth MS. has the rubric :—" Here endeþ þe tale of þe man of lawe; And here bygynneþ þe prologe of the Sqwiere ;" after which the said Prologue follows, consisting of 28 lines, and beginning : " Oure hoost vpon his stiropes stood anon." What, we may well ask, was the ultimate fate of this Prologue ? We notice, at once, that it occurs, unaltered, in the Corpus and Lansdowne MSS. ; which furnishes proof positive, that Chaucer at one time linked the Squire on to the Man of Law, and meant them to belong to the same group. In the Tables above, I denote this 'Squire's, Prologue I' by "m."

We shall find, hereafter, that Chaucer formed a new intention with regard to the Squire, and proposed to let him follow the Merchant. The proof of this must be deferred for the present ; but it will be found later on in its due place. After forming this new intention, he had to disconnect what he had at this time connected ; and in order to see how this was done, we turn to ll. B 1163–90 in the scheme next after the Lansdowne, i.e. in the Harleian scheme, and we there find an exceedingly strange result. We find some of the lines indeed, but not all ; the 28 lines have shrunk to 22 (they would have been 23 if the scribe had not missed a line).

There is now no rubric at the end of the Clerk's Tale. There is no name to what had been the Squire's Prologue, and it ends suddenly, with the rather absurd remark : " Here endith þe man of lawe his tale," which looks like a wild note of a puzzled scribe. But, most important of all, we now no longer find, in B 1179, the remark—" Seide the Sqwier "—as in Petw., Corp., and Lansdowne ; but only—"Sayde the Sompnour." That statement can hardly have come from Chaucer, since this Prologue should properly end with—" þer is but litel Latyn in my mawe ;" whereas we are expressly told concerning the Sompnour that, when he became at all excited—" Than wolde he speke no word but Latyn." And of course the Somnour's

Prologue occurs elsewhere, not only in the Hengwrt MS. and the rest, but in the Harleian MS. itself.

I can only suppose that Chaucer, after dissociating this Prologue from the Squire, hardly knew what to do with it; and, if he left it standing, as is possible, he left the name of its speaker *blank*, on speculation. If he really thought of the Sompnour, he at once saw the contradiction, so that this Prologue ceased suddenly with l. 1185, in the middle of a sentence; and was thus practically abandoned. It was either left nameless, or was given up. The scribe actually omitted 6 lines of it, and he ought to have omitted it all.

As a matter of fact, this Prologue, *except when it is a Squire's Prologue*, is extremely scarce. Dr. Furnivall has taken the extreme trouble of printing this Prologue from 22 MSS. Of these, 18 assign it to the Squire; 3 only to the Sompnour, viz. the Harleian, Rawl. Misc. 1133, and Royal MS. 17 D xv; and one only to the Shipman, viz. Arch. Selden B 14.

On the strength of the evidence of this last MS., it has been called the Shipman's Prologue and much has been made of it. It is obvious that it was assigned to the Shipman in this MS. for no other reason than because the Shipman's Tale followed the Man of Law, owing to the eccentric arrangement (or disarrangement) of the Tales which this peculiar MS. exhibits. I do not object to its being made into a Shipman's Prologue, because, as he wants a Prologue and the Prologue suits him, it is the best thing to do with it. But it remains clear, nevertheless, that if we are to go by evidence, it was never assigned to him by Chaucer himself, but only by this single scribe and by Tyrwhitt.

The discussion of the history of this Prologue has been a digression; and it is far better to consider each scheme separately, and one at a time. I have digressed in this instance in order to show that the history of any link or prologue can be traced, and because it is an instance presenting some difficulty. The result is, briefly, that it does not appear in the Hengwrt MS.; that, in Petworth, it was written as a Prologue for the Squire, and so remained in the Lansdowne scheme; that in the next, or Harleian scheme, the Squire was otherwise provided for, and his name was then removed from the Prologue, leaving it nameless and useless, because it now preceded the Wife of Bath! And this is why it rightly disappeared altogether from the edited MSS. of the Ellesmere type. See p. 193 of the print of the Harleian MS.

But the only right way of estimating the Petworth type is by taking it as a whole; and this I now proceed to do.

There are certain links, which require distinct symbols, in order to indicate where they occur. The symbols which I shall use are these.

m = the new Squire's Prologue in Petworth (B 1163–1190).

m = the nameless Prologue in the Harleian MS.; the same lines, but with a different function; the lines, in fact, which Y have just discussed.

n = the Merchant's Prologue in the Hengwrt and Petworth schemes (F 673–708); suppressed in Lansdowne.

n = Words of the Franklin in the Harleian [1] and Ellesmere; the same lines as " n," with a different function.

h = the Host-stanza of 7 lines at the end of the Clerk's Tale in the Hengwrt scheme; suppressed in Petworth,[2] Lansdowne, and Harleian; and needlessly revived in Ellesmere.

x + y = the Franklin's Prologue (x), together with the rest of the Franklin's Prologue (y), in the Hengwrt and Petworth schemes; missing in Lansdowne; (E 2419–2440; and F 1–8). Strictly, x + y is a single set of lines, but the Six-text treats them as separable quantities, though not one of the MSS. separates them.[3]

$x + y$ = the Squire's Prologue in the Harleian and Ellesmere schemes; the same lines as x + y, with a new function.

z = the Clerk-Merchant link (E 1213–1244); which first appears in the Harleian scheme.

[1] These 'Words' are missing in the Harleian MS., because eight leaves are here lost; (but as I show below) this MS. here agrees with the Ellesmere, and the lines in question were in it originally. See p. 24.

[2] That is to say, in most of the MSS. of this type; but it occurs in Harl. 7333, Harl. 1758, Royal 18 C ii, and Barlow 20.

[3] The connexion of x and y is strikingly shown in the MSS. which, like Barlow 20, corruptly turn the lines E 2427–F 6 into a couple of seven-line stanzas, to follow the "Host-stanza;" and make *can* rime with *am*. See Specimens prefixed to the Six-text, col. 54. Tyrwhitt says that these lines are in none of the old editions, and that he was the first to print them.

e = the Epilogue to the Nun's Priest; only found in 3 MSS.; one of the Petworth type, and two of the Ellesmere type; but genuine.

With these additions, the proper description of the Hengwrt type becomes :—

1. 3. 9*a*. 2. 5*a* n 4*b* x + y 5*b*. 8*a*. 4*a* h. 6. 7. 9*b*.

The proper description of the Petworth type becomes :—

1. 2 m 5*a* n 4*b*. 3. 4*a* x + y 5*b*. 8. 6. 7 e. 9*a* 9*b*.

This shows three additions, viz. m (the Squire's Prologue, no. I), preceding 5*a* (the Squire); e (the Nun's Priest's Epilogue, in one MS.); and 8*b* (the Canon's Yeoman). And there is one suppression, viz. of h (the Host-stanza).

Only two of these are of consequence. First, the Squire's Prologue I; it forms a link between 2 (Man of Law) and 5*a* (the Squire); a link perfectly real and intentional, though afterwards broken through and left useless. The other addition is that of the Canon's Yeoman, completing Group 8.

We should also take notice, that the suppression of the Host-stanza made it easier to link the Clerk (4*a*) to something else; it is here linked to the Franklin, but it was ultimately linked to the Merchant.

Another variation requiring immediate attention is this. The Manciple's Tale is now moved down so as to precede the Parson, forming and completing Group 9. As this arrangement was never afterwards disturbed, we have no authority for dividing this group into two parts, as is only done in the Hengwrt MS. and in MSS. in which the Tales are unarranged.

RESULTS.—The Petworth MS. forms two new groups, both temporary, viz. Man of Law and Squire and Merchant, and Clerk and Franklin; and one new permanent group, viz. Manciple and Parson.

By far the most important characteristic of the MSS. of this type is that they preserve and extend a group which had already been formed in the Hengwrt MS., though it was, in the very next scheme, destroyed. This is the one expressed by 5*a* n 4*b*; *i. e.* the Squire-Merchant group, linked together by means of "n," which in Hengwrt and Petworth is called the Merchant's Prologue; and now further linked to the Man of Law. Whenever we find this arrangement, viz. "Man of Law, Squire's Prologue, Squire, Merchant's Prologue, Merchant," we may be quite sure that we have before us either a MS. of the Petworth type, or one that is founded upon it in all essentials.

It should be noted that this is by far the largest class of MSS., as might have been expected; for it is Chaucer's first "arranged" edition, and must have been eagerly sought after.   Judging by Dr. Furnivall's tables, the following MSS. belong to the set, viz. Petworth, Harl. 7333, Harl. 1758, Sloane 1685, Royal 17 D xv, Royal 18 C ii, Camb. Mm. 2. 5, Barlow 20, Laud 739, New College, and Rawlinson Poet. 149.   Probably Hatton 1, Rawl. Misc. 1133, Camb. Ii. 3. 26, Trin. Coll. Cam. R. 3. 15, and the Lichfield MS. are founded upon MSS. of the Petworth type.

At least four of these, viz. Petworth, Sloane 1685, Royal 18 C ii, and Laud 739 abruptly end the Sompnour's Tale with D 2158; but this is a mere defect, as the Hengwrt MS. gives the missing portion.   See Furnivall's Temporary Preface, p. 24.

The Petworth MS. omits the stanza in E 1170–6; so also do some other MSS. of this type, as Reg. 18 . C . ii, Sl. 1685, Harl. 1758.

The Scheme of Tales in the Lansdowne MS.

The two good MSS. known as the Corpus and Lansdowne MSS., show an arrangement of the Tales which does not differ much from the preceding or Petworth scheme, from which it is easily evolved.   That the alteration was intentional appears from the fact that there is at least one considerable improvement.

I first repeat the Petworth scheme, viz.—

      1. 2 m $5a$ n $4b$. 3. $4a$ x + y $5b$. 8. 6. 7 e. 9.

From this the Lansdowne scheme is easily evolved.   All that it does is to suppress " n " and " e," and to place $4b$ after $4a$. Hence the Lansdowne scheme is—

      1. 2 m $5a$. 3. $4a$. $4b$. [x + y] $5b$. 8. 6. 7. 9.

The suppression of " n," which was temporary, enabled its function to be changed, as the Harleian scheme, in which it reappears, will demonstrate.

The great gain was the formation of the new group $4a$. $4b$. or $4ab$; that of the Clerk-Merchant.   This was so satisfactory that, in the next scheme, a new and indissoluble link (z) was expressly written to connect them.   The sequence $4a$ z $4b$ then became Group 4.

The only other point that calls for remark is the sequence : x + y 5*b* (the Franklin's Prologue and Tale).

If we turn to what was at that time a Franklin's Prologue (x + y), as in Petworth, viz. E 2419–2440 and F 1–8, we do not find it in the Corpus and Lansdowne MSS. But it does not follow that it was suppressed; for it so happens that in both those MSS. and in Sloane 1686 the preceding Merchant's Tale has been mutilated at the end, which might account for the omission otherwise. All that we can say for certain is that this passage was not lost, for it reappears in the next scheme, in which it still follows the Merchant's Tale, though it performs a new function.

RESULTS : The old Man-of-Law-Squire group, connected, as in Petworth, by " m," remains unaltered. By the suppression of " n," the temporary junction of 5*a* (Squire) with 4*b* (Merchant) was definitely dissolved. By the placing of 4*b* (Merchant) immediately after 4*a* (Clerk), a good preparation was made for the establishment of a permanent Group 4. There are at least three MSS. of this type, viz. Corpus, Lansdowne, and Sloane 1686.

I add a note that Petworth accidentally omits B 3764, and F 1147–8. It should be noticed that the very same lines are absent from both Corpus and Lansdowne. See other examples of omissions below, at pp. 33–36.

THE SCHEME OF THE TALES ACCORDING TO THE HARLEIAN MS.

The Lansdowne scheme was shown to be as follows—
1. 2 m 5*a*. 3. 4*a*. 4*b*. [x + y] 5*b*. 8. 6. 7. 9.

The Harleian scheme results from this chiefly by help of one shifting, viz. that of 5*a* so as to follow 4*b*. At the same time, the functions of " m " and " x + y " were changed (becoming *m* and *x* + *y*); the link " z " appears for the first time ; and " n " reappears as *n*.

The resultant scheme is—
1. 2 *m*. 3. 4*a* z 4*b* *x* + *y* 5*a* *n* 5*b*. 8. 6. 7. 9.

The results are interesting and important, and are again due to the author. Let us examine them in order.

First, as to " *m*." In the last scheme, this was the Squire's Prologue, connected with the preceding Man of Law ; it has now

EV. CANT.   C become a nameless or discarded Prologue, and was either to be dropped or to be used in a new connexion. It was reduced to this condition by the shifting down of $5a$; but whatever loss accrued from its abandonment was more than compensated for elsewhere.

As I have already said at p. 13, Dr. Furnivall has printed a large collection of specimens, no less than twenty-two, of this " Man-of-Law's End-Link." Of these, as many as eighteen have the reading Squire (proving that it is a reading not to be overlooked); only three (the Harleian, Rawl. Misc. 1133, and Royal 17 D xv) read Sompnour; and only one (Arch. Selden B. 14) has Shipman. If we remove the name of the Squire, we have the Sompnour and the Shipman to choose between. I have said that it is most likely that Chaucer left a blank in place of any name, and that these names were supplied by the scribes. A contradiction is avoided in the Harleian MS., by leaving this Prologue incomplete; it stops short at the end of B 1185 without completing the sentence. On the other hand, the reading "Shipman" would suit very well, and was actually adopted by Tyrwhitt, whom Dr. Furnivall has here followed. Yet only one MS. has this reading, and at the same time makes the Shipman's Tale come next in order; whereas the Harleian MS., the best authority, makes eleven Tales intervene between this Prologue and the Shipman, showing that the idea of using it as a Shipman's Prologue could never have occurred to Chaucer. The fact that *no* final arrangement was ever arrived at by the author is thus clearly emphasised. The Harleian MS. practically preserves a now nameless or an abandoned prologue after the Man of Law.

Next, as to the sequence $4a$ z $4b$. Here $4a$ is the Clerk's Tale, and $4b$ is the Merchant's Tale. They are now for the first time connected by the excellent and well-known lines, beginning "Weping and wailing, care, and other sorwe" (E 1213–1244). That this was a satisfactory and final arrangement is obvious; and no more need be said, unless it be worth while to add that, as far as the external evidence goes, this was the latest addition to the Canterbury Tales. It wholly superseded the "Host-stanza."

The sequence $x + y$ $5a$ n $5b$. requires especial attention and respect. It is a great improvement. Hitherto, "x + y" had been a Franklin's Prologue (E 2419–2440, and F 1–8). It is called in the Six-text a Merchant's End-link and a Squire's Head-link, and is arbitrarily divided into two parts. This arbitrary division is against all the evidence, for the MSS. always keep them together. What had once been a Franklin's Prologue when the Franklin followed the Merchant or the Clerk has now become a Squire's Prologue following the Merchant. It is only the function of the lines that has changed, but not their position or their use. The object in all the schemes was to link the Merchant (or, in the Petworth scheme, the Clerk) to whatever followed ; and we must beware of deciding against Chaucer's own handiwork, in a case where he has taken all necessary pains. When we come to consider $5a$ n $5b$, we find that n is a new form of "n," which was a Merchant's Prologue in Hengwrt and Petworth. It was suppressed or is missing in Lansdowne, but in the Harleian it forms a connexion between the Squire and the Franklin, which are now joined together. This completes Group 5.

RESULTS.—The old Squire's Prologue has been dissociated from the Squire. The new link "z" now connects the Clerk with the Merchant, and consolidates Group 4. The old Franklin's Prologue $(x + y)$ has become a Squire's Prologue, following Group 4 ; and the link n connects $5a$ and $5b$, and completes Group 5. Moreover, Groups 4 and 5 are really connected, as has been shown ; so that Groups 4 and 5 are really *one*.

This Harleian scheme is the latest one that shows Chaucer's hand. In it, he succeeded in reducing the sequence $4a$ z $4b$ $x + y$ $5a$ n $5b$ into one compact whole, which we may denote by $4 + 5$. The scheme, in fact, can be briefly expressed by : 1. 2 *m*. 3. 4 + 5. 8. 6. 7. 9. ; forming *eight* Groups only. By *m* is meant the nameless or abandoned Prologue, once a Squire's, which can hardly be said to belong to the scheme at all.

It is remarkable that this, the final scheme, as far as Chaucer is concerned, is also the scarcest. I have a note that the same order of Tales appears in one of the printed editions, viz. that by Wynkyn de Worde, in 1498. MS. Laud 600 is somewhat like it, but absurdly places 2 between $4a$ and $4b$.

THE SCHEME OF THE ORDER OF THE CANTERBURY TALES
ACCORDING TO THE ELLESMERE AND CAMBRIDGE MSS.

The order of Tales in the Harleian MS. has become much
simpler; it gives us 8 Groups in the following order, viz.—

1. 2. 3. 4 + 5. 8. 6. 7. 9.

The Ellesmere MS. alters the order to the following, viz.—

1. 2. 3. 4 + 5. 6. 7. 8. 9.

It remains to collate the Harleian and Ellesmere MSS.
throughout, to see if there is any difference beyond the above
unimportant shifting.

We shall find a few points of difference, all of which can be
best explained by supposing that the Ellesmere MS. presents an
"edited" text, *i.e.* one due to some scribe or editor, and not to
the author himself; whereas there is no reason why Chaucer did
not himself suggest or authorise all the schemes that precede it;
to the exclusion, of course, of all such MSS. as fail to represent
such schemes faithfully. Only Chaucer could have reduced a
long sequence into the single group 4 + 5, at the same time
adding the fine lines in E 1213–1244.

It is simplest to copy Mr. Bradshaw's remarks, and to explain
their meaning. "Marks of an Edited Text of the Canterbury
Tales:—Gamelyn cut out. Link after Man of Law cut out.
Host-stanza inserted. Second Nun and Canon's Yeoman shunted
down late. Modern instances in Monk's Tale, at the end."—
Furnivall, Temporary Preface, p. 24. To which we may add—
revival of the Nun's Priest's Epilogue.

1. Gamelin. This tale is, of course, not Chaucer's, but he
doubtless intended to employ the material for his Yeoman's
Tale, and it was convenient to have a copy at hand. It was
not in the Hengwrt MS., but appears in the Petworth, Lansdowne, and Harleian schemes alike. I conclude that the
material was thus kept in hand for possible use; but a careful
editor, understanding how matters stood, would rightly omit it.

2. Link after Man of Law. This refers to the now so-called
Shipman's Prologue (B 1163–1190). It had once been a Squire's
Prologue, as in the Petworth, Corpus, and Lansdowne MSS.
But when, in the Harleian scheme, the Squire was placed further
on and joined to the Franklin, it became, as I have explained

at p. 13, a nameless Prologue. It is suitable for the Shipman, and
one MS. alone possesses a rubric that so calls it. But there is
no proof whatever (but clear proof to the contrary) that
Chaucer put it to any use himself; and a careful editor might
well be justified in omitting it.

3. Host-stanza inserted. This Host-stanza is the genuine
single stanza of seven lines which appeared at the end of the
Clerk's Tale in the Hengwrt MS. and in some of the MSS. of
the Petworth type, but was superseded by the Prologue of
the Merchant's Tale in the Harleian scheme (E 1213–1244).
It was therefore a mistake to preserve it; but no doubt this
was done because it was seen to be genuine.

4. Second Nun and Canon's Yeoman shunted down; i. e.
Group 8 placed between 7 and 9, whereas in all previous
schemes it had occupied a position between 5 and 6. Nothing
was gained by this; it was a matter of no consequence. I have
suggested below (at p. 22) an editorial reason for doing it.

5. Modern instances in the Monk's Tale placed at the end.
It can hardly be doubted that Chaucer's first draught of the
Monk's Tale did not include the four examples, viz. of the two
Pedros, of Visconti, and of Ugolino of Pisa, which are quite
distinct from the rest. But he was afterwards moved to com-
pose these, and naturally added them quite at the end; as the
Hengwrt MS. so distinctly shows us. But when in the Petworth
scheme, Chaucer added 20 new lines (B 3961–80) to the Nun's
Priest's Prologue, he made a pointed allusion in B 3972—"He
spak how Fortune couered was with a clowd "—to what had *once*
(before the addition of the modern instances) been the last
line of the Monk's Tale; and he easily set the matter right
by lifting up those four short lives to an earlier position in
the Tale. This arrangement was meant to be final, and is found,
accordingly, in the Lansdowne and Harleian schemes. But the
editor of the Ellesmere type of MSS. actually put this wrong
again, evidently in order to arrange the lives so as to assume
a chronological order. We can understand his obvious motive;
but we see at the same time that the arrangement was not
Chaucer's own, as all the preceding arrangements had been.
Chaucer no longer superintended his work, so that the Ellesmere
arrangement was naturally the latest. Of course other arrangements are found, but they are all unauthorised and usually due

to a mixture of types. There are, as it were, five authorised collections; the Hengwrt, the Petworth, the Lansdowne, the Harleian, and the Ellesmere; four of them due to the author (though the *first* was meant to be for purely *private* and temporary use, and was imperfectly arranged) and the fifth to a reasonable editor. MSS. that represent none of these types need not be respected for the purpose of arranging the Tales, however valuable their readings may well happen to be.

Before concluding this notice of the Ellesmere MS., I must add that MS. Camb. Dd. 4. 24 and MS. Addit. 5140, which are both of the Ellesmere type, revive the scarce Epilogue to the Nun's Priest's Tale, which is only otherwise known as being found in MS. Royal 17 D xv, which appears to be of the Petworth type. I have no doubt that Chaucer meant it to be suppressed.

I would also suggest that the apparently meaningless shifting down of Group 8 probably arose from the notion of placing the mention of Boughton-under-Blee (G 556) nearer to that of the Blee in H 3. This was a natural thing for an editor to do, especially if he had not really seized the fundamental idea that the Harleian scheme was so far from being final, and even from any approach to being final, that there was nothing really to be done but to *let it alone*. If anything is to be done to it at all, it is with regard to *m*, the nameless Prologue. It is absolutely useless where it is; but might serve for a Shipman's Prologue, if it be clearly understood that such a use is entirely unauthorised.

Other MSS. of the Ellesmere type are Camb. Dd. 4. 24, and Addit. 5140. MSS. Camb. Gg. 4. 27 and Bodley 686 are closely allied.

COMPARISON OF THE TYPES.

Now that each scheme has been considered separately, it may be useful to repeat them in order. I omit the Tale of Gamelin.

HENGWRT : 1. 3. 7*b**. 9*a*. 2. 5*a* n 4*b* x + y 5*b*. 8*a*. 4*a* h. 6. 7*a*. 9*b*.
(unarranged). See pp. 10, 15.

A. PETWORTH : 1. 2 m 5*a* n 4*b*. 3. 4*a* x + y 5*b*. 8. 6. 7(e). 9.   P. 15.

B. LANSDOWNE : 1. 2 m 5*a*. 3 4*a*. 4*b*. [x + y] 5*b*. 8. 6. 7. 9.   P. 16.

C. HARLEIAN: 1. 2 m. 3. $4a$ z $4b$ $x + y$ $5a$ n $5b$. 8. 6. 7. 9. Note that $4a$ z $4b$ $x + y$ $5a$ n $5b$ simply make up $4 + 5$. There are only 8 groups; which (omitting m) may be written simply as: 1.ʳ2. 3. 4, 5. 8. 6. 7. 9. See p. 17.

C*. ELLESMERE: 1. 2. 3. $4a$ (h) z $4b$ 5. 6. 7* (e). 8. 9; or (omitting h and e): 1. 2. 3.. 4, 5. 6. 7*. 8. 9. See p. 20.

The meanings of the symbols are here repeated, as follows: 1 (Prologue, Knight, Miller, Reeve, Cook); 2 (Man of Law); 3 (Wife, Friar, Sompnour); $4a$ (Clerk); $4b$ (Merchant); $5a$ (Squire); $5b$ (Franklin); 6 (Doctor, Pardoner); 7 (Shipman, Prioress, Sir Thopas, Melibee, Monk, Nun's Priest); 7* (the same, but with a wrong change of order in the Monk's Tale); $8a$ (Second Nun); $8b$ (Canon's Yeoman); $9a$ (Manciple); $9b$ (Parson).

Also: m (old Squire's Prologue), changed to m (nameless Prologue); n (old Merchant's Prologue), changed to n (Words of the Franklin); x + y (Merchant's End-link and Franklin's Head-link, really a Franklin's Prologue), changed to $x + y$ (Merchant's End-link and Squire's Head-link, really a Squire's Prologue); h (Host-stanza after Clerk); z (new Clerk-Merchant link); e (Nun's Priest's Epilogue).

As the Harleian MS. affords the only *authorised* order, it is best to give it in words: 1 (Prologue, Knight, Miller, Reeve, Cook); 2 (Man of Law); m (nameless Prologue); 3 (Wife, Friar, Sompnour); 4, 5 (Clerk, Merchant, Squire, Franklin); 8 (Second Nun, Canon's Yeoman); 6 (Doctor, Pardoner); 7 (Shipman, Prioress, Sir Thopas, Melibee, Monk, Nun's Priest); 9 (Manciple, Parson).

In the Six-text, these groups correspond to A; B 1–1162; m (B 1163–1190); D; E, F; G; C; B 1191–4636; H, I. Only 8 groups, not 9; since E is joined to F, and H to I.

A more correct arrangement would have been: **A**; **B** (B 1–1162); **C** (D); **D** (E, F); **E** (G); **F** (C); **G** (B 1191–4636); **H** (H, I.)

It is right to add that, though the Harleian MS. gives the right order, *i. e.* as far as order went, it is a bad specimen of its type, and has lost several lines. These are: A 2013–2018, 2039, 2958, 4355, 4358, 4375–6, 4415–22; B 417, 1175, 1186–90; D 575–584, 605–12, 619–626, 717–20; E 2356–7; *gap in the MS.*, F 617–1223; F 1455–6, 1493–8; G 155, 210–216; C 299, 300, 305–6, 478–9; B 1355, 1376–9, 2253–4, 2265, 2433, 2445,

2526, 2623–4, 2647, 2709, 2731, 2742, 2754, 2855, 3035, 3213–20, 4136–7, 4479–80; not considering omissions in the Parson's Tale. The only omission that here calls for comment is the gap of 8 leaves at the end of **E** and the beginning of **F**; for I have said above (p. 14, note) that **E** and **F** are here conjoined. Fortunately, this admits of proof; for the arrangement must have been precisely the same as in the Ellesmere MS., by help of which we know that the number of missing lines (F 617–1223) is 608; and as each leaf of the Harleian MS. usually contains 76 lines, eight such leaves would contain 608 lines also; showing complete coincidence between these MSS. at this point.

By help of the tables which I have now given, it is easy to state the exact origin and ultimate fate of every grouping and of every link. Such a history I proceed to supply.

HISTORY OF THE GROUPS.

Group 1. Never altered : the Cook's Tale was never finished; and the Yeoman's Tale, founded upon the Tale of Gamelin, was never written.

Group 2 (Man of Law). This depends on the history of "m." In the Hengwrt MS. the Squire follows, but there is mere juxtaposition; the Squire is not linked to the Man of Law. But in Petworth a new link was written to connect these Tales, entitled a Squire's Prologue, and produced a Man-of-Law-Squire-Merchant group. In the Lansdowne, the Merchant was dropped. But in the Harleian the Squire was placed after the Merchant and before the Franklin, and linked to both of them, whilst the Man of Law now stood alone. This destroyed the value of m; it became m (a nameless Prologue), and Tyrwhitt proposed to assign it to the Shipman, as is accidentally done in a single MS. which is ill arranged.

Group 3 (Wife, &c.). Always a distinct group in every scheme.

Groups 4 and 5 (Clerk, Merchant, Squire, Franklin). Hengwrt has 5a. n. 4b. x + y. 5b; $i. e.$ Squire, Merchant, Franklin, in a single group; the Merchant being linked by " n," at this time a Merchant's Prologue, to the Squire; and linked by " x + y," a Merchant's End-link and Franklin's Head-link (more correctly a Franklin's Prologue) to the Franklin. But 4a, the Clerk, stands alone, after 8a (Second Nun).

In Petworth, 5a. n. 4b remains, i.e. we have still a Squire-Merchant group; but it is now linked to 2 preceding it, and the new group is a Man-of-Law-Squire-Merchant group. At the same time, the Clerk precedes The Franklin's Prologue (E 2419–2440, F 1–8) and Tale; and is linked to it by peculiar readings in E 2420 and E 2425. In the former of these lines, the phrase " euel wyves " alludes to those addressed in the Envoy to the Clerk's Tale. Other MSS. rightly have " swiche a wyf," because in them the allusion is to the wife mentioned in the Merchant's Tale. As to E 2425, see pp. 32, 33.

In Lansdowne, we have only a Man-of-Law-Squire group. The Merchant is placed after the Clerk, but there is, as yet, no Clerk-Merchant link. This gives the arrangement: Man-of-Law-Squire; Group 3 ; Clerk ; Merchant ; Franklin. Whether the Merchant was linked to the Franklin we cannot say; for the Merchant's Tale is mutilated at the end in all of the three MSS. of this type.

In the Harleian, the Man of Law is severed from the Squire, and becomes a group by itself ; at the same time, the old Squire's Prologue becomes useless.

But the Clerk-Merchant group is definitely formed by help of a new Clerk-Merchant link ; thus making group 4 complete. At the same time, group 5 has been placed after it ; so that the sequence now becomes Clerk-Merchant-Squire-Franklin, all fairly linked together. For the very same Franklin's Prologue (x + y = E 2419–2440, F 1–8), which was used in Petworth to succeed the Clerk, now becomes a Squire's Prologue, succeeding the Merchant. This is a point which it is almost impossible to follow in the Six-text edition, because the head-lines above these lines (E 2419–2440, F 1–8) are not suitable to all the MSS. Thus the Petworth extract is named, at p. 476, the " Merchant's End-link," and at p. 478, the " Squire's Head-link," though the MS. says, at the beginning, " The prologe of the Fraunkeleyn," and at the end, " Here endeth the prologe of the Fraunkeleyn ; " and it has nothing to do with either the Merchant or the Squire. That it cannot be a " Merchant's End-link " appears from the fact that the preceding Tale is that of the Clerk. Of course these very useful titles or headlines—such as the " Merchant's

End-link"—are intended for general purposes, without referring
to the peculiarities of each particular MS.; and I only note that
the title given does not always apply, in order to warn the reader
that it is best to refer to the tables at pp. 2, 3.

Group 6 (Doctor, Pardoner) is independent of the rest.

Group 7 (Shipman, Prioress, Sir Thopas, Melibee, Monk, Nun's
Priest) is really all one, and well linked together. But it will be
found that, in several MSS., the continuity of the group is broken,
owing to the irresponsibility of scribes.

By the symbol 7* I mean that the four "modern instances"
in the Monk's Tale come at the end of the Tale. This happens
only in the Hengwrt MS. and in MSS. of the Ellesmere type;
perhaps there are just a few exceptions.

Group 8 (Second Nun, Canon's Yeoman) is incomplete in the
Hengwrt MS.; in all the rest it is complete and self-contained.

Group 9 (Manciple, Parson) is really but one group. The two
Tales were at first separate, as in the Hengwrt MS., but were
soon afterwards joined together, and so remained.

The rather numerous complications are really due to the shifting function of the links; and the results can only be shown at
once by means of tables.

GENUINE REJECTED LINES.

It will be seen that, in the course of his work, Chaucer had
occasion to reject some of the lines which he had once intro-
duced. The chief examples are: (1) the Host-stanza, superseded
by the Harleian Clerk-Merchant link; (2) the *first* Squire's
Prologue, which should not have appeared in the Harleian MS.,
where it is wrongly preserved as a tag to the Man of Law's
Tale; and (3) the Nun's Priest's Epilogue, which, if it had not
been revived by the Ellesmere editor, would only have been
known as occurring in a single MS. All are genuine, but were
meant to be suppressed. The Host-stanza was actually suppressed in the first (or Petworth) recension; and Chaucer seems
to have been contemplating its suppression even when the
Hengwrt MS. was prepared; for he repeats the third line of it
—"Me were leuere than a barel ale" near the end of that MS.
in the form—"I hadde leuere than a barel ale;" B 3083.

6. 5*b*. 9.   In other words, Group 3 again comes before Group 7, and thus the very MS. which is selected to set everything right agrees with all the rest in making Sittingbourne precede Rochester. I submit that this ought to be final; and that, instead of considering what Chaucer ought to have done, we have rather to consider what he actually did.

It would appear, in fact, that the results to be obtained from the MSS. themselves are, even at the best, quite unsatisfactory. Any improvement must be purely editorial; and I am quite willing to acquiesce, as I have always done, in Dr. Furnivall's proposal to utilise the "nameless" prologue as a Shipman's Prologue, and to join on to it not only that Tale itself, but all those that belong to the same Group.   We are all most grateful for his Six-text edition, and for his edition of the Harleian MS.; and it will readily be understood that the present paper entirely depends upon these seven printed texts, and upon the excellent tables of contents of MSS., as prefixed to the Six-text edition.   In particular, I wish to record my gratitude to him for taking the precaution, when printing the MSS., of giving the numbers of their leaves.   For this is the only safe guide to the order in which each of them arranges the Tales.

It remains to be said that several MSS. have been neglected, because they exhibit the Tales in an order which cannot be fitted into any scheme whatever.   Some of these may have arisen from a contamination of types, the scribe making use of two or more copies as he could best come by them.   It is not worth while to particularise them, as they afford us no assistance as regards arrangement.   But even these it is possible to group together by the internal evidence of the readings which they exhibit: and all the MSS. have accordingly been successfully arranged into seven groups by Dr. Koch, to whose Introduction to the Pardoner's Tale it suffices merely to refer.

THE BLACK-LETTER EDITIONS.

The most important of the black-letter editions is Thynne's, from which several succeeding editions are derived.   Thynne follows in the main the Petworth type; but he had access to an edition or MS. of the Harleian type also, because he inserts the

Clerk-Merchant link, which occurs in that type only. It follows that his edition shows no distinct variety of type, and is useless for our present purpose. The complete formula for Thynne's edition is : 1. 2. m. 5*a*. n. z. 4*b*. 3. 4*a*. h. 5*b*. 8. 6 (with a spurious prologue), 7 * (with a spurious prologue), e. 9. It bears some resemblance, (in arrangement, hardly in all the readings) to Caxton's first edition, which, as Caxton admitted, was not very good.

Tyrwhitt points out a blunder of Thynne's, which is extremely instructive. He gives, just before the Merchant's Tale, both the Words of the Merchant to the Squire (F 673–708), in which the Merchant complains of his son's undutiful conduct, and the Clerk-Merchant link (E 1213–1244), in which the same Merchant says that he has been married only two months ! He has, in fact, combined " n " in Petworth with " z " in the Harleian. It is true that both are Merchant's Prologues, but *they belong to different types !*

Caxton's first edition is certainly of a mixed type, and does not help us. It agrees with Lansdowne in suppressing " n," but admits " z," as in the Harleian. The order of stories in the Monk's Tale follows that in the latter MS.

The order in Caxton's second edition agrees with none of the MSS. described by Dr. Furnivall ; for it makes the Merchant follow the Man of Law, and the Second Nun follow the Clerk ! Both the editions by Pynson follow suit. But the edition by Wynkyn de Worde in 1498 actually follows the Harleian scheme.

A Note on the Petworth MS.

I think it would be premature to consider the possible effects of the preceding investigation on the choice of readings in passages where the MSS. differ. It will certainly enable us in some cases to see what the readings mean, which is the first step to deciding upon the reading to be adopted

I take, as an example, the readings of E 2425, which occurs in a rather Protean link which I have called " x." We can most easily explain the readings by taking them in their practically chronological order. Heng. has : " By this Marchantes Tale it preueth weel." There is here no difficulty, because the reference is direct, viz. to the Merchant's Tale that precedes.

But in the Petworth MS., such a reference would be quite unsuitable, because the preceding tale is that of the Clerk. And the reading is: "By mony ensaumples it preueth well." The scribe cannot be quite right, because the line will not scan. I think he has left out the word *olde*; at any rate, *well* should be *weel*, and the reading: "By mony ensaumples [olde] it preueth weel" is probably correct.

The context shows that the Host is lamenting the abundance of evil wives, who are always busy to deceive unfortunate men; as proved, he says, by many examples. If we take notice that the preceding tale is the Clerk's, we see at once that there is here a perfectly fitting reference to the Clerk's Envoy, in which the author recommends wives to refrain from imitating the example of Griselda, and gives special hints to arch-wives, slender wives, fair wives, and ugly wives, as to their manipulation of their husbands. It shows, in fact, that when, in the Petworth scheme, what was then the Franklin's Prologue followed the Clerk's Envoy, the author's intention was to connect the Franklin with the Clerk.

But in the Lansdowne scheme, this is again changed; the Merchant again precedes the Franklin, and the Hengwrt reading might very well have been restored. We cannot certainly say if this was then done, because the three MSS. of the Lansdowne type are here imperfect. But the Harleian MS. actually restores the original reading, which the Ellesmere MS. also preserves.

The point of this note is to the effect that, although the Petworth MS. has, in this line, a different reading from the Hengwrt, the Lansdowne, and the Ellesmere, it is nevertheless correct. For the reading which is suitable for those MSS. would have been quite unsuitable for its own arrangement of the Tales. The same remark applies to E 2420, where Petworth again has a line of its own, as has been already noted at p. 25.

Some Omissions and Insertions.

The above investigation gives the relative priority of the various types of MS. It is worth saying that the order of types

Ev. Cant.   D above given is perfectly consistent with the various omissions, insertions, and peculiar readings that here and there occur.

It is obvious to any one that consults the MSS. that there is a connexion of the closest kind between the Hengwrt and Ellesmere MSS.; and we now know in which direction the borrowing lies. The Ellesmere is of the latest type, and is an edited MS.; and it is clear that the editor had access to a "Hengwrt" MS., which was one of his most important sources. Amongst other things, a very close agreement in the spelling often extends through many consecutive lines. Again, the Ellesmere MS. abounds in side-notes, many of which appear to have come from Chaucer himself. The same notes appear, in the same places, in the Hengwrt MS., whence they are carefully copied.[1]

Consistently with this, we find that the Ellesmere and Cambridge MSS. sometimes follow the Hengwrt MS., where all the rest vary.

Another source of the Ellesmere MS. was a MS. of the Harleian type, which it sometimes follows as against all the rest.

It also appears that whilst the Corpus and Lansdowne MSS. are very nearly of the same type, the form of the Corpus MS. is somewhat older, and agrees more closely with the Petworth than the Lansdowne does.

I now enumerate the chief omissions, etc., in the Hengwrt MS.

This MS. alone contains two extra lines in the Prologue, viz. A 252b, and A 252c. These lines were afterwards lost, possibly by accident. On the other hand, it omits A 637–8.

The Hengwrt MS. omits A 2681 and 2682, in the Knight's Tale, and the Ellesmere and Cambridge follow suit. But the other types retain them.

The Hengwrt MS. omits four lines of Arcite's last speech (A 2779–82). They were doubtless added afterwards.

The Hengwrt MS. omits two lines in the Miller's Prologue (A 3155–6). They do not appear in the Petworth, nor in the Lansdowne. But they appear in the Harleian, and were thence copied into the Ellesmere.

The lines A 3721–2 are in Ellesmere and Cambridge only,

---

[1] There are some exceptions. Thus, in A 1955, 1956, the former *see* is glossed in Heng. by *ad vid.* (*i.e.* it is the *verb*), and the latter by *i. mare* (*i.e.* it is the *substantive*). The Ellesmere misses this. So also in A 2298.

among the seven MSS. But they are also in Thynne's edition, which contains a mixture of types.

It is only the Hengwrt MS. that records the fact about the Cook's Tale, that " Of this Cokes Tale maked Chaucer na moore." This is highly significant. It really means that, at a comparatively early stage, Chaucer definitely and finally abandoned it.

What is now called the Shipman's Prologue (B 1163–1190) first appeared as a Squire's Prologue in the Petworth MS. The Hengwrt does not contain it at all. It was imperfectly retained by mistake in the Harleian.

A line in Sir Thopas (B 1995) was accidentally dropped in the Hengwrt MS., and actually disappeared in nearly all later copies. A line which serves the purpose appears in MS. Reg. 17 D xv ; but it may have been concocted. It does not appear in Thynne.

Three lines in Sir Thopas (B 2042–4) were omitted in the Petworth MS., and hence do not not appear in the Corpus and Lansdowne. They were restored (but badly) in the Harleian, which was undoubtedly influenced by some revised MS. of high authority that has unfortunately been lost.

In Melibeus, B 2252–3, a passage was omitted in Hengwrt. It is consequently omitted in all other copies. The same thing occurs twice more, further on ; see B 2623–4, and B 2854.

In the Monk's Tale, the stanza concerning Adam is not in Hengwrt. Neither is it in Corpus. But the rest have it.

In the Nun's Priest's Prologue, it is particularly to be noted that Hengwrt omits 20 lines (B 3961–3980) ; and Petworth and Corpus follow suit. They appear in Lansdowne, Harleian, and Ellesmere. It is highly significant ; for these are the lines in which the Knight refers to what the Monk has said—" He spak how ' fortune covered with a cloude I noot never what.' " This proves quite clearly that the idea of bringing the story of Crœsus to the end of the Tale was an afterthought. It was done forcibly, by inserting the modern stories at an earlier place.

In the Nun's Priest's Tale, Petworth omits B 4233–8. So do Corpus and Lansdowne.

In the Doctor's Tale, Ellesmere omits C 103–4. In the Words of the Host, Hengwrt and Petworth (followed by Ellesmere)

omit C 297–8. In the Pardoner's Tale, the spurious lines
C 487*b* and 488*b* appear in Corpus and Lansdowne only.

In the Wife of Bath's Preamble, several lines occur in
Ellesmere and Cambridge only; viz. D 575–84, 609–12, 619–26;
and 717–20 in Ellesmere only. All four passages are in
Thynne. There is no significance in the omission by Petworth
of D 2159–2294; for the lines are found in Hengwrt as well as
elsewhere.

The Merchant's Prologue, E 1213–44, first appears in the
Harleian MS. It is absent from Hengwrt, Petworth, and
Lansdowne (and from Corpus).

In the Merchant's Tale, E 1305–6, where Hengwrt is imperfect,
there is much variation in the readings.

In several places, MSS. of all types omit lines owing to
confusing lines that end alike. Even the Ellesmere, which
seldom errs thus, has lost E 1358–61, which the rest retain.

Petworth omits E 1927–8; so do Corpus and Lansdowne.

Corpus and Lansdowne omit the end of the Merchant's Tale,
E 2319–2440; and also F 1–8. This is a troublesome loss.

In the Franklin's Tale, certain lines are absent from Petworth,
Corpus, and Lansdowne; viz. F 1147–8, 1191–6, 1423–4, 1433–4.
F 1567–8 appear in Petworth, but not in the other two.

F 1455–6 and F 1493–8 appear in Ellesmere only; though
F 1455–6 are found in Thynne.

In the Second Nun's Tale, Petworth, Corpus, and Lansdowne
twice omit a clause, viz. in G 213–4 and G 432–3.

The Canon's Yeoman's Tale is absent from the Hengwrt MS.,
as has been already said.

It thus appears that each type often affected the one that
succeeded it. On the other hand, the Harleian and Ellesmere
types often restore what had previously been lost.

The preceding remarks refer to the seven chief MSS. *only*.
Collation with other MSS. may easily modify some of them.

I venture to think that, even in the totally different matter of
collating the various readings, it will never do any harm to look
at the seven MSS. in this particular order, viz. **Hengwrt, Petworth,
Corpus, Lansdowne, Harleian, Ellesmere, Cambridge**. I have
tried the experiment in several places, and have found that some
light is sometimes thrown upon the matter by this very simple
proceeding.

A very curious example occurs in the Knight's Tale, A 2037—
" As is depeynted in the sterres above." That *sterres*, i.e. stars,
is the right reading is certain ; for there is a parallel passage in
B 194—" For in the *sterres*, clerer than is glas, Is writen," etc.
Yet the scribe of the Hengwrt MS. very oddly spelt the word
sertres, making the *t* the fourth letter instead of the second : and
so producing a ghost-word.[1] The remarkable point is, that
Petworth has *certres*, with *c* for *s* ; Corpus and Lansdowne have
sertres ; Ellesmere has *certres* ; and Cambridge has *sertres* ; so that
all these practically follow suit.   Only the Harleian, which is so
often independent of the rest, has the right spelling *sterres*.   And
at the same time the carelessness of the Harleian scribe is well
exemplified by the fact that he drops the preceding *the*.

[1] If the *er* in *sterres* be represented, as often, by a mere curl, it would
appear as " st'res."   If a careless scribe's eye was attracted by this curl,
he might read it as " s'tres," by anticipation.   But this is " sertres."